United States Government Accountability Office

Report to Congressional Committees

I0448672

July 2013

JUSTICE GRANT PROGRAMS

DOJ Could Improve Decision-Making Documentation and Better Assess Results of DNA Backlog Reduction Program Funds

GAO-13-605

GAO Highlights

Highlights of GAO-13-605, a report to congressional committees

JUSTICE GRANT PROGRAMS

DOJ Could Improve Decision-Making Documentation and Better Assess Results of DNA Backlog Reduction Program Funds

Why GAO Did This Study

Since 2008, Congress has appropriated more than $100 million each year to the Department of Justice (DOJ) that may be used, among other things, to reduce DNA backlogs and enhance crime laboratory capacity. NIJ, within DOJ, is responsible for, among other things, providing awards for DNA analysis and forensic activities. NIJ's DNA Backlog Reduction Program was established to provide grants to state and local governments with the intent, in part, of reducing the backlog of DNA samples. The conference report accompanying the Consolidated and Further Continuing Appropriations Act, 2012, mandated GAO to examine, among other things, DNA analysis funds. This report addresses (1) how NIJ has allocated its DNA and forensic program appropriation over the past 5 fiscal years, (2) the extent that NIJ has a process to determine its funding priorities for its DNA and forensic program appropriation, and (3) the extent that NIJ verifies data on grant results submitted by grantees and measures the outcomes of the DNA Backlog Reduction Program. GAO reviewed relevant appropriations, NIJ funding documentation, and data from fiscal years 2008 through 2012, and interviewed NIJ officials.

What GAO Recommends

GAO recommends that NIJ clearly document the rationale for annual funding priorities, develop a cost-effective approach to verify the reliability of grantee performance data, and revise its performance measure to reflect actual completed cases. DOJ agreed with GAO's recommendations and outlined steps to address them.

View GAO-13-605. For more information, contact Michele Mackin at (202) 512-4841 or MackinM@gao.gov.

What GAO Found

The National Institute of Justice (NIJ) allocated funding for various DNA and other forensic science activities, with the majority of the available $691 million from fiscal years 2008 through 2012 going to state and local governments to reduce the DNA backlog. Specifically, over this 5-year period, 64 percent was allocated through initiatives that directly benefit state and local efforts to reduce DNA backlogs and build DNA analysis capacity. The largest initiative was NIJ's DNA Backlog Reduction Program, and other DNA backlog initiatives included DNA analysis of cold cases, among others. A smaller portion (31 percent) went to other forensic sciences initiatives, such as research and development and training, although NIJ officials stated that funding these initiatives may have long-term benefits for reducing the DNA backlog. The remainder of the funding went toward other activities, such as management and administration.

NIJ has a process in place to determine DNA and forensic program funding priorities, but its decisions regarding these priorities are not clearly documented. According to NIJ officials, the rationale for funding the DNA Backlog Reduction Program versus other initiatives is documented in briefing slides, but these documents do not show NIJ's rationale for how funding priorities are determined. For example, while the budget documents for fiscal years 2012 and 2013 show the final amounts NIJ decided to allocate to various initiatives, these documents do not provide details on the justifications for how funding levels were determined for each initiative. Without a clearly documented process that demonstrates the rationale for NIJ's annual funding priorities, there is limited transparency regarding how and why the agency is allocating its funding.

NIJ could verify data and revise its performance measure to better assess the DNA Backlog Reduction Program. NIJ assesses performance of this program by requiring grantees to submit reports every 6 months that, in part, outline their progress in meeting program goals and objectives. However, NIJ does not have an approach to verify the reliability of the data—testing data to ensure data quality—and as a result, faces continuing data errors. Verifying these data would help ensure that the data are reliable enough to show that the program is successfully meeting its goals. In addition, NIJ has a performance measure to assess the results of this program—percent of reduction in DNA backlog casework—but it is a projection of DNA casework that grantees expect to complete as opposed to an actual tabulation of completed cases. While measuring annual performance for multiyear grants can be challenging because the completed number of cases is not known until after the grant period closes, taking steps to analyze performance data on actual cases completed could help NIJ to better assess actual results.

Contents

Figures

Abbreviations

DOJ	Department of Justice
GMS	Grants Management System
GPRA	Government Performance and Results Act
NIJ	National Institute of Justice
OJP	Office of Justice Programs
OMB	Office of Management and Budget
TWG	Technology Working Group

July 31, 2013

Congressional Committees

Since 2008, Congress has appropriated more than $100 million each year to the Department of Justice (DOJ) that may be used to reduce DNA backlogs and enhance crime laboratory capacity. Among other things, these funds are intended to be used for DNA analysis and capacity enhancement, as well as other forensic activities, such as research and development in crime scene blood spatter or footprint impressions. The Office of Justice Programs (OJP), established by the Justice Assistance Act of 1984, is the primary grant-making arm of DOJ. Within OJP, the National Institute of Justice (NIJ), the research arm of DOJ, is responsible for evaluating programs and policies that respond to crime, and providing and administering awards for DNA analysis and forensic activities, among other criminal justice activities.

DOJ officials have reported that while federal funding has been made available to state and local governments to reduce DNA backlogs, the demand for DNA testing continues to exceed the capacity of laboratories to process these samples. According to DOJ, the reasons for the backlog include (1) the increased amount of DNA evidence that already has been collected in criminal cases, and (2) expanded efforts by federal and state governments to collect DNA samples from convicted offenders and arrested persons. As reported by state and local laboratories funded by DOJ, NIJ estimated that in 2011—the most recent estimate—the year-end backlog for DNA evidence collected from crime scenes was approximately 91,000 cases, and additional crimes can be committed by serial offenders as analysis of evidence is delayed. NIJ's DNA Backlog Reduction Program (DNA Backlog Reduction Program) provides grants to state and local governments with the intent, among other things, of reducing the backlog of DNA samples.[1]

In making appropriations to DOJ for "DNA-related and forensic programs and activities," Congress has specified the amounts to be obligated for

---

[1]Grantees of this program can use funding to analyze cases containing DNA evidence or can analyze samples of DNA evidence taken from convicted offenders or arrested individuals, or both, in accordance with state laws. Grantees may also use funds to increase laboratory capacity.

specific programs and activities. For example, DOJ has been directed to use a large portion of the funds for "a DNA analysis and capacity enhancement program and for other local, State, and Federal forensic activities, including the purposes authorized under section 2 of the DNA Analysis Backlog Elimination Act of 2000 (the Debbie Smith DNA Backlog Grant Program)." Throughout this report, we refer to these latter funds as the 'DNA and forensic program appropriation.'

The conference report accompanying the Consolidated and Further Continuing Appropriations Act, 2012—appropriating funds for DOJ and various other agencies—mandated GAO to examine the use of funds awarded for DNA analysis and capacity enhancement for the past 5 years.[2]

To carry out the mandate, we addressed the following questions:

- How has NIJ allocated its DNA and forensic program appropriation over the past 5 fiscal years?
- To what extent does NIJ have a process to determine its funding priorities for its DNA and forensic program appropriation?
- To what extent does NIJ verify data on grant results submitted by grantees and measure the outcomes of the DNA Backlog Reduction Program?

To determine how NIJ allocated DNA and forensic program funds, we reviewed relevant appropriations from fiscal years 2008 through 2012 and compared related NIJ expenditures and award data for the same time period.[3] Specifically, to determine the amount of the appropriation that went to DNA backlog reduction purposes or other forensic science purposes, we reviewed NIJ awards and expenditure data using DOJ and OJP financial systems that track expenditures, OJP's electronic system for grant management, and hard copies of awards not contained in the electronic grant system. Using the awards' purpose statements, we

---

[2]H.R. Rep. No. 112-284, at 247 (Conf. Rep.). During the time period of our review from fiscal years 2008 through 2012, Congress appropriated funds for other programs that related to DNA analysis in state and local units of government. However, the scope of this review focused only on the specific appropriation available for "DNA analysis and capacity enhancement."

[3]We included in our definition of "DNA and forensic program appropriation" amounts for fiscal years 2008 through 2012, although the appropriation language for fiscal year 2008 differed to some extent.

categorized the awards into those used for DNA backlog reduction purposes, other DNA-related efforts and those used for other forensic sciences purposes. We then solicited and incorporated input from NIJ officials to verify how we categorized each award. We assessed the reliability of these data by conducting electronic testing of the data and interviewing NIJ's managers responsible for the data. We determined the data were sufficiently reliable for the purposes of determining how NIJ allocated DNA and forensic program funds.

To determine the extent to which NIJ has a process to determine funding priorities for its DNA and forensic program appropriation, we reviewed NIJ documentation outlining NIJ's annual process for determining annual funding priorities. The available documentation consisted of briefing slides for fiscal years 2008 through 2011 and budget memos for fiscal years 2012 and 2013. We also interviewed NIJ officials knowledgeable about the agency's annual funding priority process. We compared NIJ's processes with requirements for documenting key decisions outlined in the Standards for Internal Control in the Federal Government.[4]

To determine the extent to which NIJ verifies data on grant results submitted by grantees and measures the outcome of its DNA Backlog Reduction Program, we reviewed NIJ performance information collected from grantees from fiscal years 2008 through 2012 used to assess the results of this program, as well as guidance NIJ provided to grantees on reporting performance data. We also reviewed OJP policies and guidance outlining monitoring requirements for assessing grantee progress and performance. To gain a better understanding of NIJ's monitoring efforts, we reviewed monitoring documents for a sample of 11 awards—including 8 grants, 1 contract, and 2 interagency agreements[5]—to include different NIJ-funded efforts, such as the DNA Backlog Reduction Program and other forensic science efforts. Although our review of this sample cannot be generalized to all of NIJ's monitoring efforts, it helped to inform our understanding of NIJ's efforts to assess results and measure performance. We also interviewed NIJ officials responsible for assessing

---

[4]GAO, *Standards for Internal Control in the Federal Government,* GAO/AIMD-00-21.3.1 (Washington, D.C.: November 1999).

[5]Grants are provided to eligible entities, such as state and local governments, to conduct DNA analysis or research, among other things. Contracts are official agreements with various non-government entities to perform services. Interagency agreements are awards provided to other federal agencies.

performance and outcomes of the DNA Backlog Reduction Program. We compared NIJ's efforts with OJP data reporting requirements[6] for complying with the Government Performance and Results Act of 1993 (GPRA).[7] We also compared NIJ's efforts with requirements for verifying data and assessing performance outlined in Office of Management and Budget guidance, GPRA, and our prior work.[8]

We conducted this performance audit from June 2012 to July 2013 in accordance with generally accepted government auditing standards. Those standards require that we plan and perform the audit to obtain sufficient, appropriate evidence to provide a reasonable basis for our findings and conclusions based on our audit objectives. We believe that the evidence obtained provides a reasonable basis for our findings and conclusions based on our audit objectives.

Background

OJP's bureaus and offices provide grants and other awards to various organizations, including state and local governments, universities, and private entities, which are intended to develop the nation's capacity to prevent and control crime, administer justice, and assist crime victims. Within OJP, NIJ serves as DOJ's research and development agency and provides evidence-based knowledge and tools to address crime and justice challenges, particularly at the state and local levels. As part of this mission, NIJ provides awards from the DNA and forensic program appropriation and administers these awards for the purpose of DNA analysis and capacity enhancement and for other forensic science

---

[6]Department of Justice, Office of Justice Programs, Office of the Chief Financial Officer, *2011 Financial Guide* (Washington, D.C.: July 2012).

[7]Pub.L.No. 103-62, 107 Stat. 285, as amended by the GPRA Modernization Act of 2010, Pub. L. No. 111-352, 124 Stat. 3866. Under GPRA, agencies are required to hold programs accountable to Congress and the public by establishing performance goals, identifying performance measures used to indicate progress toward meeting the goals, and using the results to improve performance as necessary.

[8]Office of Management and Budget, Circular No. A-11: *Preparation, Submission, and Execution of the Budget,* (Washington, D.C.: August 3, 2012); GAO, *Executive Guide: Effectively Implementing the Government Performance and Results Act,* GAO/GGD-96-118 (Washington, D.C.: June 1, 1996); *The Results Act: An Evaluator's Guide to Assessing Agency Annual Performance Plans,* GAO/GGD-10.1.20 (Washington, D.C.: April 1998); *Performance Plans: Selected Approaches for Verification and Validation of Agency Performance Information,* GAO/GGD-99-139 (Washington, D.C.: July 30, 1999).

purposes. Within NIJ, the Office of Investigative and Forensic Sciences is responsible for administering awards for these purposes. According to OJP, approximately seven NIJ staff members within the Office of Investigative and Forensic Sciences are responsible for managing and monitoring funds associated with the DNA and forensic program appropriation.

Funding Mechanisms

NIJ prioritizes initiatives it will fund from the DNA and forensic program appropriation on an annual basis and provides awards through various funding mechanisms, including grants and nongrant agreements as described below. NIJ's award mechanism varies depending on the type of initiative being funded and the type of recipient receiving the funds.

- Grants[9]
  - **NIJ formula discretionary grants:** Awards provided under a formula set by DOJ and based primarily on the violent crime rate. The DNA Backlog Reduction Program[10] is the only formula grant program awarded through the DNA and forensic program appropriation.[11]
  - **Other discretionary grants:** Awards provided to eligible entities, which vary depending on the purpose and requirements of the

---

[9]During the period of this review, from fiscal years 2008 through 2012, the vast majority of grants provided by NIJ through this appropriation were a form of grant called a cooperative agreement. Cooperative agreements are similar to grants, the primary difference being that cooperative agreements include substantial involvement by the agency in carrying out the activity in the agreement. See 31 U.S.C. § 6305. For the purposes of this report, we refer to these agreements as grants.

[10]The purposes of the NIJ DNA Backlog Reduction Program were generally similar to the purposes of section 2 of the DNA Analysis Backlog Elimination Act of 2000 (the Debbie Smith DNA Backlog Grant Program, codified at 42 U.S.C. § 14135) had during the fiscal years we reviewed. During that period, the authorizing language for the Debbie Smith DNA Backlog Grant Program provided authority to DOJ to make grants to state and local governments for several different purposes, and directed DOJ to award specific percentages of the funds for certain of these purposes; for example, 40 percent was to carry out DNA analyses of samples from crime scenes. 42 U.S.C. § 14135 (a)(2), (c)(3). However, because the DNA and forensic program appropriation did not appropriate funds under the authorization for the Debbie Smith DNA Backlog Grant Program, these directives did not apply and DOJ was not required to award a specific percentage of available funds to the NIJ DNA Backlog Reduction Program or for any purpose specified in the statute for the Debbie Smith DNA Backlog Grant Program.

[11]The formula is set by DOJ and is based primarily on the violent crime rate in each state from 2 years prior to the grant's award.

award. Such grants may be awarded to state and local governments, public and private universities, as well as for-profit and nonprofit organizations. NIJ's other discretionary grants are generally awarded on a competitive basis.[12]

- Nongrants
  - **Interagency agreements:** Awards between federal agencies establishing an agreement for projects that may cover similar topics and initiatives as NIJ's other discretionary grants. Federal agencies may not receive funds through grants; however, they may compete for some awards, if eligible, or receive non-competitive awards, if determined to be appropriate for NIJ's DNA and forensic science activities.
  - **Contracts:** Agreements with various nongovernment entities, such as private laboratories, for various services, such as conducting certain DNA analytical services or providing other technical scientific services.

NIJ funds grants through solicitations, which are formal requests for funding proposals outlining goals, eligibility requirements, and the instructions for applying to receive grant funding. Federal agencies may apply under such solicitations if eligible; however, in such cases, NIJ awards federal agencies funds through interagency agreements, and not through the solicitation and grant-making process. Contracts are not funded through the typical grant-making process, but through requests for contract proposals. For the purposes of this report, "initiatives" include all awards NIJ funded from the DNA and forensic program appropriation, including awards funded through grants, interagency agreements, and contracts.

Initiatives

NIJ provides funds under various initiatives for the purposes of reducing the DNA backlog and for other forensic sciences needs, including research and development and forensic science training. Table 1 describes NIJ's initiatives funded from fiscal years 2008 through 2012

[12]NIJ's policy also allows for non-competitive awards when (1) only one applicant can perform the work of the proposed award; (2) the NIJ director has determined in writing that urgent, or other compelling, circumstances exist that make it in the public interest to make an award non-competitively; (3) a funding recipient is specified by an appropriations act or other applicable law; and, (4) recommendations in congressional reports, accompanying an appropriations act or other law, recommend an award to a particular recipient, and an award may be made consistent with applicable law, including any applicable executive orders.

through the DNA and forensic program appropriation that directly benefit state and local government DNA-related efforts to reduce backlogs and build capacity. Throughout this report, we refer to these initiatives as the DNA backlog initiatives.

Table 1: National Institute of Justice DNA and Forensic Program Initiatives Funded to Directly Benefit State and Local Government Efforts to Reduce the DNA Backlog and Build Laboratory Capacity, Fiscal Years 2008-2012

Initiative	Description of DNA backlog initiative
Formula discretionary grant funding	
DNA Backlog Reduction Program	Awards available to state and local units of government to, among other things, reduce the backlog of DNA samples for criminal justice purposes. Such awards may provide funding for technicians to work overtime and to obtain DNA analysis supplies, among other things. Funding amounts are based primarily on the violent crime rate in the state from 2 years prior to the grant's award, with each state receiving a minimum amount.
Other discretionary backlog funding	
Convicted Offender and/or Arrestee DNA Backlog Reduction Program	Awards provided to eligible states to analyze DNA samples from certain convicted offenders and arrestees to be uploaded to the National DNA Index System maintained by the Federal Bureau of Investigation that stores DNA profiles to enable laboratories to compare these profiles from DNA samples collected during the investigation process nationwide.
	This program ended during fiscal year 2010 and was subsumed into the DNA Backlog Reduction Program in 2011.
Solving cold cases with DNA	Awards provided to states and local units of government to identify, review, and investigate violent crime cold cases that have the potential to be solved using DNA analysis. A cold case refers to any unsolved criminal case for which all significant investigative leads have been exhausted.
Using DNA to identify the missing	Awards to assist eligible entities in performing DNA analysis on unidentified human remains and samples from family members of missing persons, or to help identify missing persons.
Forensic DNA unit efficiency improvement	Awards provided to states and local units of government to perform studies for implementing novel, capacity-enhancing technologies and processes into their DNA laboratories.
Convicted offender private lab analysis	Contracts provided directly to private laboratories to assist states in reducing their convicted offender and arrestee DNA sample analysis backlogs. Contracts are administered by the Office of Justice Programs.

Source: GAO analysis of NIJ information.

Table 2 describes NIJ's additional initiatives funded through the DNA and forensic program appropriation that do not directly benefit the state and local government DNA analysis backlog, but address other DNA and forensic science challenges identified by the agency from fiscal years 2008 through 2012.

Table 2: National Institute of Justice DNA and Other Forensic Sciences Initiatives That Do Not Directly Benefit State and Local Governments in Reducing the DNA Backlog, Fiscal Years 2008-2012

Initiative	Description of forensic sciences initiative
Research, development, and evaluation	Awards to provide qualified entities funding to conduct basic or applied scientific research to increase knowledge of forensic science disciplines, including but not limited to DNA analytical methods. Funding is also used to evaluate current forensic science processes and programs, including the technical aspects of DNA analysis as well the practical effects of current forensic science policy on the criminal justice community.
Forensic science training	Awards to provide educational opportunities to state and local practitioners in forensic science disciplines, including relevant criminal justice partners. Such areas of forensic science include DNA analysis, trace evidence such as explosives detection, and pattern evidence such as ballistics identification, among others.
Centers of excellence	Awards provided to qualified entities to provide technical and scientific support to crime laboratories, law enforcement, and other criminal justice agencies. Such support includes testing, evaluation, technology assistance and other services.
National Missing and Unidentified Persons System (NamUs) project and support	Awards provided to support the development, administration, and management of NIJ's NamUs system, a national data repository and resource center for missing persons and unidentified decedent remains. The database is available to states and local units of government as well as the general public.
Technical assistance	Awards provided to support elements of NIJ's mission related to forensic science for activities such as support for DOJ's criminal justice research website, providing scientific editorial activities, and providing forensic science education to policymakers to help them address the modern use of DNA analysis to improve the administration of justice.
Meetings and conferences	Funding considered a part of technical support for practitioners at the state, local, and federal levels to hold forensic science related summits. According to NIJ officials, such meetings and conferences are instrumental in developing communities to help adopt new forensic science methods among practitioners.

Source: GAO analysis of NIJ information.

Monitoring

OJP policy directs that monitoring be performed to assess the performance of programs that support NIJ initiatives. For example, for grants, during programmatic monitoring,[13] grant managers review qualitative information (such as progress reports submitted by grantees and supporting documentation on grantee program implementation), and

---

[13]Assessing programmatic progress and performance of a grant is one type of monitoring activity within OJP's overall monitoring program. Other types of monitoring include financial monitoring—to review financial aspects of a grant award and grantee—and administrative monitoring—to review compliance with grant terms and conditions, among other requirements. Programmatic and financial monitoring are carried out through communication with the grantee, desk reviews (reviews of documents in grantees' files to, among other things, assess grantee performance), and in-depth monitoring (consisting of site visits and enhanced programmatic desk reviews, which enable program managers to follow up on any issues identified during desk reviews).

quantitative information (such as performance measurement data submitted by grantees), to determine grant progress and performance. In grant applications, grantees are required to propose grant goals that support NIJ's stated program purpose, the activities through which they aim to achieve those goals, and an implementation plan describing timelines and steps for the activities. For interagency agreements and contracts, OJP and NIJ officials determine the type of monitoring documents, such as progress reports, required based on the goals and objectives of each specific award.

NIJ Has Allocated Funding for Various DNA and Other Forensic Science Activities, and the Majority Goes Directly to Reducing the DNA Backlog

From fiscal years 2008 through 2012, Congress appropriated approximately $691 million to NIJ to provide grant and other awards for state and local governments to reduce the DNA backlog and increase DNA lab capacity, as well as for other forensic science purposes.[14] The appropriations language was broad and enabled NIJ to allocate funding for a variety of forensic programs at funding levels established by the agency.[15] As a result, NIJ allocated funds for both its DNA backlog initiatives and other forensic science initiatives based on NIJ's mission and annual budgeting priorities. For instance, over the 5-year period, NIJ provided funding through the DNA Backlog Reduction Program, other discretionary DNA backlog initiatives such as analyzing DNA samples from cold cases, and other forensic science initiatives awarded through grants and nongrants including research, development, and evaluation; forensic science training; and support for the development of best practices.

---

[14]NIJ's available allocation for awarding grants and nongrants does not constitute the entire appropriation because OJP initially assesses amounts for OJP-wide management and administration, among other things.

[15]In 2008, the statutory language differed to some extent; within the appropriation for "DNA related and forensic programs," a certain amount was specified "for a DNA analysis and capacity enhancement program including the purposes of section 2 of the DNA Analysis Backlog Elimination Act of 2000. . ." Consolidated Appropriations Act 2008, Pub. L. No. 110-161, 121 Stat. 1844, 1910 (2007). Unlike the appropriations language for the subsequent years of our review, this provision did not also state that funds were available "for other local, state, and Federal forensic activities." According to officials from OJP's Office of the General Counsel, the statute lacked clarity but was reasonably read to give the agency authority to permit the use of funds for non-DNA forensic purposes. These officials told us they had discussed this issue with congressional appropriations staff at that time, and in 2009, the appropriations language explicitly included authority to provide funds for both "a DNA analysis and capacity enhancement program" as well as "other . . . forensic activities."

NIJ allocated the majority—about 64 percent, or $442 million of the available $691 million in the DNA and forensic program appropriations—to DNA backlog initiatives. Our analysis of the data shows that about $343 million of this $442 million was awarded through the DNA Backlog Reduction Program, and the remaining approximately $98 million was awarded through its other DNA backlog initiatives.[16] According to NIJ officials, these awards directly affected the DNA backlog by providing funds to state and local entities for either analyzing DNA samples or increasing the capacity of state and local laboratories to conduct DNA sample analyses.[17] Additionally, NIJ awarded approximately 31 percent, or $212 million of the available $691 million, to other DNA and forensic science purposes that do not directly reduce the DNA backlog. NIJ officials stated that funding from some of these initiatives may have indirect or long-term benefits for reducing the DNA backlog. The remainder of the funding, $38 million, went toward other activities, such as management and administration.[18] See figure 1.

---

[16]Amounts related to the DNA Backlog Reduction Program ($343 million) and other DNA backlog initiatives ($98 million) do not equal $442 million because of rounding.

[17]A small portion of awards were provided to entities other than state and local governments. For instance, NIJ awarded about $3 million of grants to for-profit companies to supplement state and local efforts to identify missing persons through DNA analysis. In addition, NIJ awarded about $3 million in contracts to for-profit companies to analyze convicted offender and arrestee DNA samples collected by state and local governments.

[18]Specifically, the remaining $38 million of the $691 million appropriated went to management and administration of OJP activities; was transferred pursuant to statute to other research and statistics accounts; or went to adjustments, such as a statutory rescission of prior-year unobligated balances. Amounts related to DNA backlog initiatives ($442 million), initiatives that do not directly reduce the DNA backlog ($212 million), and other remaining expenditures ($38 million) do not equal $691 million because of rounding.

Figure 1: Allocation of Funding of DNA and Forensic Program Appropriations for Initiatives and Other Costs, Fiscal Years 2008-2012

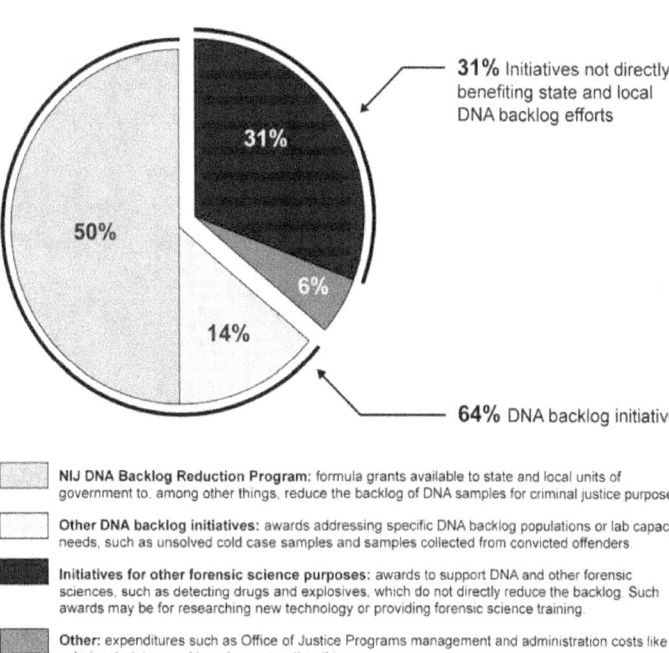

31% Initiatives not directly benefiting state and local DNA backlog efforts

64% DNA backlog initiatives

NIJ DNA Backlog Reduction Program: formula grants available to state and local units of government to, among other things, reduce the backlog of DNA samples for criminal justice purposes.

Other DNA backlog initiatives: awards addressing specific DNA backlog populations or lab capacity needs, such as unsolved cold case samples and samples collected from convicted offenders.

Initiatives for other forensic science purposes: awards to support DNA and other forensic sciences, such as detecting drugs and explosives, which do not directly reduce the backlog. Such awards may be for researching new technology or providing forensic science training.

Other: expenditures such as Office of Justice Programs management and administration costs like salaries, training, and travel, among other things.

Source: GAO analysis of NIJ grants, nongrant awards, and other appropriation information.

Note: Other expenditures included $27 million assessed for management and administration of OJP activities, about $2 million transferred to other research and statistics accounts, and about $9 million adjusted at the end of fiscal years through statutory rescissions, for example. OJP assessments are not limited to DNA and forensic program activities but may include OJP-wide costs for training, travel, and computer infrastructure. Percentages do not add to 100 because of rounding.

We further analyzed the 64 percent of appropriated funding that went toward the DNA Backlog Reduction Program and other DNA backlog initiatives over the 5-year period. We found that, annually, NIJ generally has increased the percentage of funding provided to the DNA Backlog Reduction Program, while the overall amount of the DNA and forensic program funds available through appropriations and prior year carryover decreased from a high of about $153 million in fiscal year 2010 to $118 million in fiscal year 2012.[19] For instance, in fiscal year 2008, NIJ awarded about 36 percent of the total amount available to NIJ to obligate for the DNA Backlog Reduction Program. By 2012, NIJ had increased the amount to about 63 percent of the total available for obligation. At the same time, funds awarded through its other DNA backlog initiatives generally decreased. See figure 2 for the proportion of funds provided for the DNA Backlog Reduction Program and other backlog initiatives by fiscal year.

---

[19]Annual amounts available for obligation do not necessarily equal the total amount appropriated for the 5-year period, specifically because unobligated amounts carried over to the next fiscal year may increase the amount that OJP and NIJ can obligate beyond the enacted appropriation.

Figure 2: Annual Percentage of Funds Provided for DNA Backlog Reduction Program and other DNA Backlog Initiatives, Fiscal Years 2008-2012

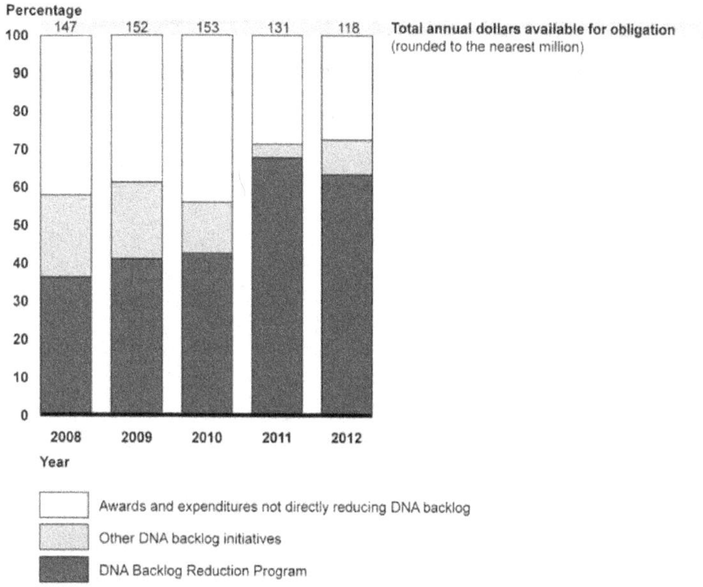

Percentage

Year	Total annual dollars available for obligation (rounded to the nearest million)
2008	147
2009	152
2010	153
2011	131
2012	118

Legend:
- Awards and expenditures not directly reducing DNA backlog
- Other DNA backlog initiatives
- DNA Backlog Reduction Program

Source: GAO analysis of NIJ grants, non-grant awards, and other appropriation information.

Note: Annual amounts available for obligation do not add to the total amount appropriated for the 5-year period of approximately $691 million because annual amounts carried over to the next fiscal year and increased the funding OJP and NIJ could obligate beyond the enacted appropriation.

NIJ officials stated that the increased funding for the DNA Backlog Reduction Program was primarily because the agency decided to prioritize the program more than its other initiatives. In addition, NIJ officials stated that funding also increased when the agency subsumed the Convicted Offender and/or Arrestee DNA Backlog Reduction Program into the larger DNA Backlog Reduction Program starting in 2011. As a result, the new program had a larger scope and provided more money to grantees through NIJ's continued emphasis on this program.

We also analyzed the breakdown of the grants and nongrant awards for other forensic science initiatives that do not directly contribute to reducing the DNA backlog.[20] From fiscal years 2008 through 2012, this amounted to about 31 percent of the $691 million appropriated, or about $212 million. See figure 3 below for an analysis of funds awarded to other forensic science initiatives.

Figure 3: Proportion of Funds Allocated for Forensic Science Initiatives not Directly Benefiting State and Local Efforts to Reduce the DNA Backlog, Fiscal Years 2008-2012

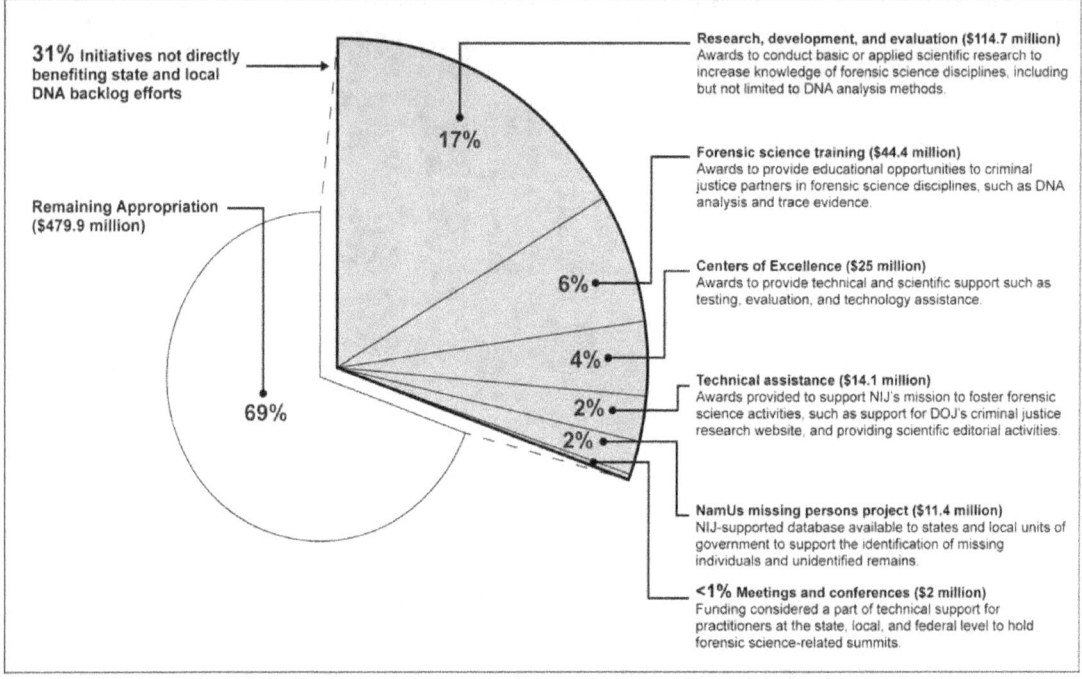

Source: GAO analysis of NIJ grants, non-grant awards, and other appropriation information.

Note: Totals are rounded to the nearest $0.1 million, and percentages are rounded to the nearest percent.

[20]Unlike DNA backlog initiatives that were awarded primarily to state and local governments, other forensic science projects have been awarded to federal agencies (through interagency agreements), for-profit companies, nonprofit groups, as well as public and private universities. For more information on other forensic awards, please see appendix I.

We further analyzed grant and award description information across the initiatives that do not directly contribute to reducing the DNA backlog to determine whether they were DNA-related, and our analysis showed that more than $121 million of the approximately $212 million for other forensic science initiatives covered a range of DNA-related projects such as research, development, and evaluation to improve the ability to analyze aged or compromised DNA samples, DNA training for state and local laboratories, and DNA-related initiatives such as the National Missing and Unidentified Persons System. NIJ officials stated that the agency funded these projects because they provide valuable services and resources to practitioners solving crimes with DNA. For instance, DNA-related research can lead to faster and better methods for recovering and analyzing DNA. Also, NIJ officials stated that the agency's mission includes facilitating faster and better DNA-related knowledge transfer across the country. As a result, several of its technical assistance initiatives covered a facet of NIJ's commitment to training and information sharing. NIJ officials stated they consider these DNA-related initiatives to be a form of DNA capacity enhancement and an important part of the strategy to reduce the DNA backlog.

The remaining amount—approximately $90 million of the $212 million—was awarded to support other areas of forensic science.[21] This represents about 13 percent of the $691 million appropriated and includes efforts such as research, development, and evaluation of faster and less expensive methods to detect drugs or explosives at crime scenes and training for cell phone and other digital information forensic evidence. NIJ officials stated that NIJ has authority to support the criminal justice community in general forensic science endeavors, which is important because lab technicians must process many types of forensic evidence. NIJ officials added that cases may be solved through many different types of evidence and manners of processing, not just through DNA. They stated that faster and better analysis of other forensic evidence may help increase the amount of time lab technicians have to analyze DNA samples and indirectly benefit how many DNA cases can be completed.

---

[21]The amounts associated with DNA-related initiatives that are not directly supporting state and local efforts to reduce the DNA backlog ($121 million) and forensic science initiatives that are not DNA related ($90 million) do not sum to $212 million in this report because of rounding.

NIJ Has a Process in Place to Determine DNA and Forensic Program Funding Priorities, but Decisions Are Not Clearly Documented

NIJ has a process in place for determining its annual priorities for the allocation of DNA and forensic program appropriation funds; however, NIJ does not clearly document this process. According to NIJ officials, NIJ staff use the prior fiscal years' funding as a starting point to make a proposed initial estimate of the amount to be allocated to the DNA Backlog Reduction Program. Specifically, NIJ staff examine the amount of funds remaining on active formula grant awards from prior fiscal years, and then use historical funding data to determine what is needed to fund eligible applicants for the next fiscal year. After the proposed initial allocation for the DNA Backlog Reduction Program has been determined, NIJ staff then develop an initial recommendation for how the estimated remaining funding will be allocated to other DNA and forensic initiatives. In addition, NIJ uses the professional expertise of its forensic staff, as well as input from NIJ-sponsored Technology Working Groups (TWG). These groups are committees of 25 to 30 experienced practitioners from local, state, tribal and federal agencies and laboratories associated with a particular NIJ technology investment portfolio, such as DNA Forensics or General Forensics, that help NIJ determine the criminal justice technology needs of the field.[22] After NIJ staff arrive at proposed allocations among the initiatives, staff brief the Director of NIJ with documents—such as budget briefing slides or funding memos—that outline their priority areas. The NIJ Director then determines the initial allocation among the various initiatives.

NIJ next begins the process of implementing these initiatives through solicitations.[23] According to NIJ officials, the solicitations are developed by NIJ staff possessing the relevant subject matter expertise, in consultation with Office of Investigative and Forensic Sciences leadership and with input from the forensic science TWGs. NIJ then posts each solicitation to the NIJ web site and either a federal government grant website or an OJP web-based system in order to accept proposals from qualified applicants

---

[22]According to NIJ officials, the DNA Forensics TWG provides input on DNA-related research and development and the General Forensics TWG provides input on forensic topics, such as crime scene investigations. There are a total of 20 TWGs. Although the TWGs provide input, according to NIJ officials, they are not tasked with or responsible for determining how to allocate funds.

[23]In addition to solicitations, NIJ implements initiatives through interagency agreements (for awards provided to federal agencies) and contracts (for agreements with various nongovernment entities).

applying for funding.[24] Qualified proposals submitted in response to a competitive solicitation are subjected to a peer review process and evaluated for their scientific merit.[25] Funding recommendations for individual proposals are, in part, informed by peer review and, in the case of forensics-related research proposals, the needs and priorities identified by the TWGs.

According to NIJ officials, the rationale for funding allocation decisions, such as the amount to be used for the DNA Backlog Reduction Program, is documented in the briefing slides and funding memos that are presented to the NIJ Director. However, according to our review, these documents do not consistently or adequately demonstrate NIJ's rationale for how funding priorities are determined. Specifically, from fiscal years 2008 through 2011, NIJ used budget briefing slides to present funding priorities to the NIJ Director. These briefing slides showed the various initiatives and the amount of funding NIJ proposed to allocate to each initiative, but they did not consistently provide justifications for how or why NIJ determined these amounts. For fiscal years 2008 and 2009, the briefing slides included rationale sections that were descriptions of the funding being allocated rather than justifications for why NIJ chose to allocate specific funding amounts to each initiative. For example, for fiscal year 2008, for the Forensic Technology Center of Excellence initiative, NIJ provided an itemized list of the funding request and projects in the rationale section. For fiscal year 2010, the budget briefing document outlined recommended changes to the DNA Backlog Reduction Program, such as adjusting minimum funding levels available to states and units of local government. However, the document did not include any rationale for this decision. For fiscal years 2012 and 2013, NIJ changed its process from using briefing slides to using funding memos to present funding prioritization decisions to the NIJ Director. While these memos show the final amounts NIJ decided to allocate to various initiatives, they do not

---

[24]The federal government grant website—Grants.gov—provides a unified electronic storefront for interactions between grant applicants and the federal agencies that administer grant funds. The Grants Management System (GMS) is OJP's web-based, data-driven, computer application system that provides end-to-end support for the application, award, and management of grants. The electronic grant files contained within GMS are the official federal grant records of OJP.

[25]With the exception of a standing peer review panel process piloted in fiscal year 2012, NIJ uses OJP's guidance—*OJP Order, OJP Grant Application Peer Reviews*—to conduct its peer review process.

provide details on the justifications for how funding levels were determined for each initiative. Further, although NIJ had a category for rationale in the fiscal year 2008 and 2009 briefing slides, this practice ended beginning with fiscal year 2010. According to NIJ officials, there was no longer a need to include a rationale in the briefing slides because the briefings to the NIJ Director began occurring later in the prioritization process and the Director's signature, indicating approval of funding prioritization decisions, had already been obtained.

Standards for Internal Control in the Federal Government states that internal control and all transactions and other significant events need to be clearly documented, and the documentation should be readily available for examination. The documentation should appear in management directives, administrative policies, or operating manuals, and all documentation and records should be properly managed and maintained. The standards also state that transactions and significant events are to be clearly documented to help management with decision making and to help ensure operations are carried out as intended.[26]

According to NIJ officials, the budget briefing slides for fiscal years 2008 through 2011 and the funding memos for fiscal years 2012 and 2013 are the only documents the agency uses to show its rationale for prioritization of the DNA and forensic program appropriation. Additionally, in light of budget uncertainty from year to year, NIJ officials believe their current process is the most useful because it allows the agency flexibility for making decisions. However, without a clearly documented process that demonstrates the rationale for how NIJ is prioritizing its DNA and forensic program appropriation, there is limited transparency regarding how and why the agency is allocating its funding. In addition, documenting the agency's rationale for prioritizing funding—regardless of the timing of the briefing to the NIJ Director—would be worthwhile so that there is a record of the agency's decision. Furthermore, the significant amount of funding NIJ administers under this appropriation, as well as the continuing demand for DNA analysis, highlights the importance of ensuring transparency when it comes to determining priorities for funding allocations.

---

[26] GAO/AIMD-00-21.3.1.

Verification of Data Reliability and Revision of Its Performance Measure Could Help NIJ Better Assess Performance of the DNA Backlog Reduction Program

NIJ has processes in place to assess progress of the DNA Backlog Reduction Program, but does not have an approach to verify performance data submitted by grantees so as to reduce error rates. NIJ also has a performance measure to assess the results of this program, but data are lacking to determine whether efforts are having a measurable impact in reducing the DNA backlog.

NIJ Assesses Performance, but Verifying Performance Data Could Help NIJ Better Assess Results

NIJ assesses performance of the DNA Backlog Reduction Program by requiring grantees to submit reports every 6 months outlining their progress in, among other things, meeting the program goals and objectives established in their initial applications for funding. A key component of these progress reports is data on grant results—performance data—that outline grantee progress such as in analyzing cases using NIJ funds. [27] NIJ program managers are responsible for reviewing performance measure data to assess progress in meeting grantee goals and objectives. NIJ also assesses grantee progress and performance by conducting monitoring activities that include, among other things, desk reviews and in-depth monitoring activities.[28]

While NIJ has developed performance measures for its grant programs and collects performance measurement data from its grantees, the agency does not have an approach to verify the reliability of the data—a process of checking or testing performance data to reduce the risk of using data that contain significant errors—and, as a result, faces continuing data errors. In October 2011, based on NIJ's review of

---

[27]Grantees of NIJ's DNA Backlog Reduction Program can use funding to analyze either DNA casework (from crime scenes) or DNA database samples (from convicted offenders or arrestee), or both.

[28]Desk reviews include a comprehensive review of materials available in the grant file to determine administrative, financial, and programmatic compliance, as well as grantee performance. In-depth monitoring consists of site visits or enhanced programmatic desk reviews (implemented in fiscal year 2011) which allow grant managers to pursue any issues identified during the desk review and assess the status of project implementation.

progress reports, NIJ noted that, with respect to the DNA Backlog Reduction Program, 30 percent of progress reports submitted by grantees in 2011 had errors in the collection and reporting of data, contained inaccurate data, or lacked goals and updates on progress achieved. Furthermore, according to an NIJ review of site visits it conducted in 2010, NIJ identified many issues with how data are collected and, many times, NIJ found data that were neither accurate nor auditable. In response to these concerns, in October 2011, NIJ provided grantees with additional guidance for preparing data collection plans and required them to explain any changes in data that they had previously submitted. NIJ also began requiring grantees to use an updated progress report form and provided an updated spreadsheet with pre-populated math formulas for reporting data on cases and samples analyzed to minimize data reporting errors. However, in March 2013, a year and a half after these actions, NIJ officials stated that they still estimate that 30 percent of progress reports submitted by grantees contain errors. NIJ officials noted that progress reports are sent back to grantees to correct mistakes, and the grantees are in turn required to send the reports back to NIJ for review and approval.

OJP requires that award recipients collect data that are appropriate for facilitating reporting requirements for GPRA, as amended, and that valid and auditable source documentation is available for such data.[29] Office of Management and Budget (OMB) guidance states that in order to assess progress toward achievement of performance goals, performance data must be appropriately accurate and reliable for intended use.[30] OMB's guidance further states that verification and validation[31] of performance data support the general accuracy and reliability of performance information, reduces the risk of inaccurate performance data, and provides a sufficient level of confidence to Congress and the public that the information presented is credible as appropriate to its intended use. In addition, our work on performance assessment has identified that data verification helps to ensure that users can have confidence in the

---

[29]Department of Justice, Office of Justice Programs, Office of the Chief Financial Officer, *2011 Financial Guide* (Washington, D.C.: July 2012).

[30]Office of Management and Budget, Circular No. A-11: *Preparation, Submission, and Execution of the Budget* (Washington, D.C.: August 3, 2012).

[31]Validation is the assessment of whether data are appropriate for a performance measure. See GAO/GGD-99-139.

GAO-13-605 DOJ DNA Analysis Grants

reported performance information because it provides a mechanism for assessing data completeness, accuracy, consistency, and timeliness, among other things.[32]

NIJ officials stated that they had not taken action to verify performance data because NIJ does not have access to original data to check that data are being reported correctly. As a result, officials stated that they primarily rely on grantees to submit reliable data. Officials also noted that they do not have the resources to systematically verify the reliability of data reported because, on average, each program manager is responsible for monitoring about 200 awards. Officials explained that as part of monitoring efforts—enhanced programmatic desk reviews, site visits, and review of progress reports—program managers will spot-check data for any anomalies and will follow up with grantees in cases where the data seem inaccurate.

Ensuring the reliability of the data is especially important in light of the fact that the DNA Backlog Reduction Program is NIJ's largest investment. Furthermore, NIJ reports performance data in OJP's annual Performance Budget to show progress in reducing the DNA backlog.[33] Without an approach to verify grantee-reported data, NIJ cannot provide assurance that grantees have valid and auditable source documentation for the data they report, as required by OJP. In addition, NIJ officials are not required to verify performance data when reviewing progress reports. NIJ estimated that 30 percent of progress reports were sent back to grantees for correction because they contained errors. However, because program managers are not required to verify performance data, NIJ cannot be certain that the remaining 70 percent of progress reports were free of data errors. As a result, NIJ cannot provide a sufficient level of confidence to Congress and the public that performance data associated with the DNA Backlog Reduction Program are reliable enough to show that the program is successfully meeting its goals or reducing the DNA backlog. As part of its site visit monitoring efforts, during which time NIJ officials

---

[32]GAO/GGD-99-139. We conducted work in six agencies and identified examples illustrating a wide range of approaches for increasing the quality, validity, and credibility of performance information.

[33]Department of Justice, Office of Justice Programs, *FY 2014 Performance Budget*, March 2013.

have access to grantees' original source data, NIJ could, for example, assess whether additional edit checks are needed to better ensure data are reliable. Although there could be a cost associated with such efforts, defining a cost-effective approach to verify its performance measurement data would better position NIJ to help ensure that it is providing quality information to the public, internal agency officials, and congressional decision makers who play a role in determining where to allocate NIJ funding resources.

NIJ's Performance Measure Includes Estimated, but Not Actual Outcomes of the DNA Backlog Reduction Program

We also found that the performance measure NIJ uses to measure results of the DNA Backlog Reduction Program may yield an incomplete picture. The performance measure, reported as "percent of reduction in DNA backlog casework," is a projection of DNA casework that grantees expect to complete as opposed to an actual tabulation of completed cases. Using data submitted by grantees, NIJ calculates the number of cases grantees expect to test with future funding, divided by the DNA casework backlog reported by grantees at the end of the calendar year. In fiscal year 2011, for example, the reported percent reduction was 32.9 percent and was based on a calculation of the estimated number of cases grantees expected to be completed, divided by the total DNA casework backlog. Grantees submit their estimated number of cases to NIJ in their funding applications before they are awarded the grants and begin work. Further, these grantees have up to 3 years to complete their work.

NIJ officials explained that reducing the DNA backlog is a DOJ goal in support of GPRA and the agency reports this measure in OJP's annual Performance Budget. According to officials, the DNA Backlog Reduction Program is NIJ's program with the most immediate impact in reducing the DNA backlog. However, NIJ's performance measure does not demonstrate actual results, as required by GPRA, as amended.[34]

In addition, NIJ has established a target of 25 percent reduction in DNA backlog casework, which NIJ officials stated that they establish based on historical knowledge. However, NIJ's target is also a projection of the DNA casework that grantees expect to achieve based on estimates submitted in grantee applications.

---

[34]See 31 U.S.C. § 1115.

Our prior work on GPRA states that agencies that were successful in measuring performance strived to establish performance measures that, among other things, enable an organization to assess accomplishments, make decisions, realign processes, assign accountability, and demonstrate results so as to tell each organizational level how well it is achieving its goals.[35] In addition, in our work assessing performance measures, we identified that performance measures should provide useful information for decision making by providing managers and other stakeholders timely, action-oriented information in a format that helps them make decisions that improve program performance.[36] Measures that do not provide managers with useful information will not alert managers and other stakeholders to the existence of problems or help them respond when problems arise.

According to NIJ officials, the agency is unable to develop a performance measure that reports actual cases completed (on the fiscal year basis called for in OJP's annual budget submission) under the DNA Backlog Reduction Program because grantees have up to 3 years to complete their work and the completed number of cases for the entire grant period is not known until the grant period closes. In addition, NIJ officials explained that they would prefer a more meaningful measure, but the current measure captures NIJ's best guess of the percentage reduction in DNA backlog casework.

While measuring annual performance for multi-year grants can be challenging, NIJ could take steps to better assess the results of DNA backlog efforts by analyzing performance data on actual cases completed, which the agency already collects from grantees every 6 months as part of the grantees' progress reports. In fact, for grants that have not yet closed, NIJ has already started analyzing actual performance data to identify grantees' annual progress in meeting goals.

---

[35]GAO/GGD-96-118.

[36]GAO, *Tax Administration: IRS Needs to Further Refine Its Tax Filing Season Performance Measures*, GAO-03-143 (Washington, D.C.: November 22, 2002). According to attributes of performance measures from various sources, such as earlier GAO work, Office of Management and Budget Circular No. A-11, and GPRA, among other sources, we identified that in order to track how programs and activities can contribute to attaining goals and missions, organizations need to have performance measures that (1) demonstrate results, (2) are limited to the vital few, (3) cover multiple program priorities, and (4) provide useful information for decision making.

Such data, once sufficiently reliable, could help NIJ to better assess actual results and develop a more accurate performance measure. Officials from OJP's Office of the Chief Financial Officer—the office responsible for reporting performance measure information—stated that in order to modify a measure, NIJ would need to propose the change and OJP would submit the proposed revised measure, with approval of other components of DOJ, to OMB in the OJP annual budget submission.

By revising its performance measure to include casework actually completed, NIJ will be better situated to provide decision makers with timely, action-oriented information that helps them make decisions that improve program performance or that alerts them to the existence of problems so they can respond to them when they arise.

Conclusions

As reported by DOJ, federal funds to address the persisting backlogs of untested DNA samples, among other things, have provided needed support to state and local laboratories to help resolve criminal cases. However, DOJ could take additional steps to improve transparency and better assess results. While NIJ has a process to determine funding priorities, documenting the agency's rationale for funding allocation decisions, as recommended by standards for internal control in the federal government, NIJ could enhance transparency of the agency's funding priorities. DOJ has a process in place, as well as a performance measure, to assess results of NIJ's DNA Backlog Reduction Program, but the agency could verify data and use actual outcomes, as required by federal requirements, to attain reasonable assurance that funds are having a measureable impact in reducing DNA backlogs.

Recommendations for Executive Action

We recommend that the Director of NIJ take the following three actions.

In order to provide stakeholders and Congress greater transparency regarding its funding allocations, we recommend that the Director of NIJ document the rationale for its annual funding priorities.

In order to assist Congress and NIJ management and stakeholders to better assess whether NIJ's DNA Backlog Reduction Program is having a measurable impact in reducing the DNA backlog, we recommend that the Director of NIJ take the following two actions:

- develop a cost-effective approach to verify performance data submitted by grantees to provide reasonable assurance that such data are sufficiently reliable to report progress in reducing the DNA backlog, and,

- revise the "percent of reduction in DNA backlog casework" performance measure to include casework actually completed as part of the measure instead of casework that is projected.

Agency Comments and Our Evaluation

We provided a draft of this report to DOJ for review and comment. DOJ provided written comments, which are reproduced in full in appendix II, and technical comments, which we incorporated as appropriate. DOJ agreed with all three of the recommendations and outlined steps to address them.

With respect to the first recommendation, OJP stated that in fiscal year 2014, the Director of NIJ will begin documenting the rationale for the estimated initial allocation of funds appropriated (or anticipated to be appropriated) for DNA analysis and capacity enhancement program efforts, and for other local, state, and federal forensic activities.

Regarding the second recommendation, OJP stated that once NIJ revises the performance measure for the NIJ DNA Backlog Reduction Program (in response to our third recommendation), NIJ will begin developing a cost-effective approach to provide reasonable assurance that data collected from grantees, in support of the new or revised performance measure, are sufficiently reliable to report program progress.

Finally, for the third recommendation, OJP stated that the Director of NIJ will undertake efforts to revise the performance measure for the NIJ DNA Backlog Reduction Program and anticipates that the new or revised performance measure will reflect actual cases competed. OJP also noted that the new or revised performance measure will be subject to review and/or approval of other DOJ components as the well as the Administration.

We are sending copies of this report to the Attorney General, appropriate congressional committees, and other interested parties. In addition, the report is available at no charge on the GAO website at http://www.gao.gov.

If you or your staff have any questions about this report, please contact me at (202) 512-4841, mackinm@gao.gov. Contact points for our Offices of Congressional Relations and Public Affairs may be found on the last page of this report. Key contributors to this report are listed in appendix III.

Michele Mackin
Director, Acquisition and Sourcing Management

List of Committees

The Honorable Barbara A. Mikulski
Chairwoman
Subcommittee on Commerce, Justice, Science, and Related Agencies
Committee on Appropriations
United States Senate

The Honorable Richard C. Shelby
Ranking Member
Subcommittee on Commerce, Justice, Science, and Related Agencies
Committee on Appropriations
United States Senate

The Honorable Frank R. Wolf
Chairman
Subcommittee on Commerce, Justice, Science, and Related Agencies
Committee on Appropriations
House of Representatives

The Honorable Chaka Fattah
Ranking Member
Subcommittee on Commerce, Justice, Science, and Related Agencies
Committee on Appropriations
House of Representatives

Appendix I: Recipients of Awards Made by the National Institute of Justice for the DNA and Forensic Program, Fiscal Years 2008 through 2012

The Department of Justice's (DOJ) National Institute of Justice (NIJ) was appropriated about $691 million from fiscal years 2008 through 2012 for the DNA and forensic program, which is administered by its National Institute of Justice (NIJ).[1] NIJ awarded almost two-thirds of all funds—or about 63 percent—to either state or local units of government from the DNA and forensic program appropriation for fiscal years 2008 through 2012, as seen in figure 4.

Figure 4: Recipients of Grants and Other Awards Funded through the DNA and Forensic Program Appropriation, Fiscal Years 2008-2012

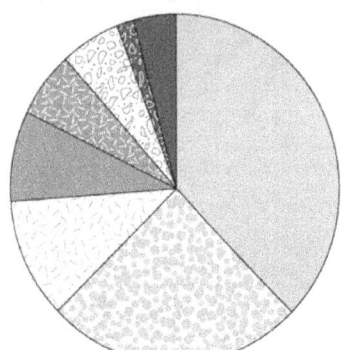

Recipient	Total dollars received (in millions)	Percentage
States	260.1	38
Local units of government	175.3	25
Public colleges and universities	76.3	11
Nonprofit organizations	57.4	8
For profit businesses	43.3	6
Other federal agencies	28.5	4
Private colleges and universities	12.3	2
Other	38.2	6
	691.5	

Source: GAO analysis of NIJ grants, non-grant awards, and other appropriation information.

Note: Totals are rounded to the nearest $0.1 million, including the total appropriation. Totals do not equal to $691 million because of rounding. "Other" includes expenditures for management and administration assessments, and adjustments, transfers, or carryovers.

Of the about $691 million, about $442 million, or 64 percent, went to directly benefit state and local units of government to reduce the DNA backlog. Of the $442 million, about 96 percent, or about $422 million, was allocated directly to either state or local units of government through NIJ's DNA backlog initiatives, including NIJ's DNA Backlog Reduction Program.

---

[1] In making appropriations to the Department of Justice for "DNA-related and forensic programs and activities," Congress has specified the amounts to be obligated for specific programs and activities. For example, DOJ has been directed to use a large portion of the funds for "a DNA analysis and capacity enhancement program and for other local, State, and Federal forensic activities, including the purposes authorized under section 2 of the DNA Analysis Backlog Elimination Act of 2000 (the Debbie Smith DNA Backlog Grant Program)." We refer to efforts funded by these latter funds as the DNA and forensic program.

A⬚en⬚⬚ ⬚⬚⬚e⬚i⬚ients ⬚⬚A⬚ar⬚s ⬚a⬚e ⬚y t⬚e
Nati⬚nal ⬚nstit⬚te ⬚⬚J⬚sti⬚e ⬚r t⬚e DNA an⬚
⬚⬚rensi⬚Pr⬚gra⬚ ⬚is⬚al ⬚ears ⬚00⬚t⬚r⬚⬚g⬚
⬚01⬚

Three percent—or about $14 million—was awarded to public universities to conduct DNA analyses and increase lab capacity on behalf of state and local governments, and an additional 1 percent—about $6 million—was awarded to for-profit businesses to conduct similar analyses for certain populations of DNA samples.

Approximately $212 million of $691 million was awarded to various entities for purposes that do not directly support state and local governments' efforts to reduce the DNA backlog, but for which there may be an indirect benefit to the reduction of DNA backlogs.[2] For example, of the $212 million, public colleges and universities received about $63 million for initiatives that do not directly benefit state and local government efforts to reduce DNA backlogs. See table 3.

⬚a⬚le 3⬚⬚e⬚i⬚ients ⬚⬚N⬚J DNA an⬚ ⬚⬚rensi⬚ Pr⬚gra⬚ A⬚⬚r⬚⬚riati⬚n⬚⬚is⬚al ⬚ears ⬚00⬚-⬚01⬚

⬚e⬚i⬚ient ⬚⬚⬚⬚n⬚s	Dire⬚tly ⬚ene⬚iting state an⬚ l⬚⬚al DNA ⬚a⬚⬚⬚g e⬚⬚⬚rts	N⬚t ⬚ire⬚tly ⬚ene⬚iting state an⬚ l⬚⬚al DNA ⬚a⬚⬚⬚g e⬚⬚⬚rts	⬚e⬚i⬚ient ⬚⬚tals
State units of government	$257,979,499	$2,145,645	$260,125,144
Local units of government	164,096,921	11,237,848	175,334,769
Public colleges and universities	13,715,861	62,603,059	76,318,920
Nonprofit organizations	—	57,400,607	57,400,607
For-profit Businesses	5,858,676	37,426,044	43,284,721
Other federal agencies	—	28,488,746	28,488,746
Private colleges and universities	—	12,270,010	12,270,010
Management and administration assessed by OJP	—	—	26,538,740
Adjustments, transfers, or carryover	—	—	11,707,855
⬚⬚tal	⬚⬚⬚1⬚650⬚95⬚	⬚⬚11⬚5⬚1⬚960	⬚691⬚⬚69⬚511

Source: GAO analysis of NIJ grants, awards, and other appropriation information.

Note: Amounts for management and administration assessments and adjustments, transfers, or carryover represent other funds that were not awarded through an NIJ initiative. Therefore, these amounts did not specifically address DNA backlog or other forensic science efforts. Amounts for categories do not equal totals because of rounding to the nearest dollar.

[2]Such purposes included initiatives such as research, development, and evaluation, and forensic science training, among others. The remaining $38 million of the $691 million appropriated went to management and administration of OJP-wide activities; was transferred pursuant to statute to other research and statistics accounts; or went to adjustments, such as a statutory rescission of prior-year unobligated balances. For specific amounts allocated to management and administration of OJP-wide activities and adjustments, transfers, or carryover, see table 3.

Appendix II: Comments from the Department of Justice

U.S. Department of Justice

Office of Justice Programs

Washington, D.C. 20531

JUL 12 2013

Ms. Michele Mackin
Director
Acquisition and Sourcing Management
Government Accountability Office
441 G Street, NW
Washington, DC 20548

Dear Ms. Mackin:

Thank you for the opportunity to review and comment on the draft Government Accountability Office (GAO) report entitled, "Justice Grant Programs: DOJ Could Improve Decision-Making Documentation and Better Assess Results of DNA Backlog Reduction Program Funds" (GAO-13-605). The U.S. Department of Justice (Department) appreciates the GAO's work in planning and conducting this review, and issuing the draft report.

The draft GAO report contains three Recommendations for Executive Action to the Department, which are restated in bold text below and are followed by our response.

1. **In order to provide stakeholders and Congress greater transparency regarding its funding allocations, we recommend that the Director of NIJ document the rationale for its annual funding priorities.**

   The Office of Justice Programs (OJP) agrees with the Recommendation for Executive Action. Beginning in Fiscal Year 2014, the Director of the National Institute of Justice (NIJ) will document the rationale for the estimated initial allocation of funds appropriated (or anticipated to be appropriated, as has often been the case) for a DNA analysis and capacity enhancement program, and for other local, State, and Federal forensic activities. Please note that the final allocations, among the various NIJ programs and activities related to DNA and other forensics, are reflected in the awards ultimately made, late in the fiscal year, and are based on such factors as: the amount of the appropriation as enacted; the needs of the forensic science community; the number and overall quality of the applications received under the various programs; and the results of rigorous peer reviews (other than in the case of the NIJ DNA Backlog Reduction Program, which is administered through an NIJ formula).

In order to assist Congress and NIJ management and stakeholders to better assess whether NIJ's DNA Backlog Reduction Program is having a measurable impact in reducing the DNA backlog, we recommend that the Director of NIJ take the following two actions:

2. Develop a cost-effective approach to verify performance data submitted by grantees to provide reasonable assurance that such data are sufficiently reliable to report progress in reducing the DNA backlog.

OJP agrees with the Recommendation for Executive Action. The Director of NIJ will develop a cost-effective approach for verifying performance data submitted by grantees under the NIJ DNA Backlog Reduction Program, in order to provide reasonable assurance that such data are sufficiently reliable to report program progress. As indicated in the response to Recommendation 3 below, OJP and NIJ also plan to revise the performance measure for the NIJ DNA Backlog Reduction Program. Accordingly, once the performance measure for the NIJ DNA Backlog Reduction Program is revised, and based on a reexamination of its current procedures for review of performance data submitted by grantees, NIJ will begin development of a cost-effective approach to reasonably assure that data collected from grantees for the new/revised performance measure are sufficiently reliable to report program progress.

3. Revise the "percent of reduction in DNA backlog casework" performance measure to include casework actually completed as part of the measure instead of casework that is projected.

OJP agrees with the Recommendation for Executive Action to revise the performance measure. The Director of NIJ will undertake efforts to revise the performance measure for the NIJ DNA Backlog Reduction Program. Subject to the review and/or approval by other components of the Department and the Administration, NIJ anticipates that the new/revised performance measure will reflect actual cases (or samples, or DNA profiles, or other pertinent work) completed under the NIJ DNA Backlog Reduction Program, and also take into consideration existing complexities such as those posed by lag times in receiving data.

If you have any questions regarding this response, you or your staff may contact Maureen Henneberg, Director, Office of Audit, Assessment, and Management, at (202) 616-3282.

Sincerely,

Karol V. Mason
Assistant Attorney General

cc: Tony West
        Acting Associate Attorney General

2

cc: Anna Martinez
Senior Advisor to the Associate Attorney General
Office of the Associate Attorney General

Mary Lou Leary
Principal Deputy Assistant Attorney General

James H. Burch, II
Deputy Assistant Attorney General
  for Operations and Management

Gregory Ridgeway
Acting Director
National Institute of Justice

Leigh Benda
Chief Financial Officer

Maureen Henneberg
Director
Office of Audit, Assessment, and Management

Rafael A. Madan
General Counsel

Charles Moses
Deputy General Counsel

Melodee Hanes
Acting Director
Office of Communications

Richard P. Theis
Director, Audit Liaison Group
Internal Review and Evaluation Office
Justice Management Division

OJP Executive Secretariat
Control Number 20130923

3

Appendix III: GAO Contact Staff and Acknowledgments

GAO Contact	Michele Mackin, (202) 512-4841, or mackinm@gao.gov
Staff Acknowledgments	In addition to the contact named above, Dawn Locke (Assistant Director), Joel Aldape, Brian Lipman, and Jeremy Manion made significant contributions to the work. Also contributing to the report were Michele Fejfar, Grant Mallie, Jessica Orr, and Janet Temko.

GAO's Mission	The Government Accountability Office, the audit, evaluation, and investigative arm of Congress, exists to support Congress in meeting its constitutional responsibilities and to help improve the performance and accountability of the federal government for the American people. GAO examines the use of public funds; evaluates federal programs and policies; and provides analyses, recommendations, and other assistance to help Congress make informed oversight, policy, and funding decisions. GAO's commitment to good government is reflected in its core values of accountability, integrity, and reliability.
Obtaining Copies of GAO Reports and Testimony	The fastest and easiest way to obtain copies of GAO documents at no cost is through GAO's website (http://www.gao.gov). Each weekday afternoon, GAO posts on its website newly released reports, testimony, and correspondence. To have GAO e-mail you a list of newly posted products, go to http://www.gao.gov and select "E-mail Updates."
Order by Phone	The price of each GAO publication reflects GAO's actual cost of production and distribution and depends on the number of pages in the publication and whether the publication is printed in color or black and white. Pricing and ordering information is posted on GAO's website, http://www.gao.gov/ordering.htm. Place orders by calling (202) 512-6000, toll free (866) 801-7077, or TDD (202) 512-2537. Orders may be paid for using American Express, Discover Card, MasterCard, Visa, check, or money order. Call for additional information.
Connect with GAO	Connect with GAO on Facebook, Flickr, Twitter, and YouTube. Subscribe to our RSS Feeds or E-mail Updates. Listen to our Podcasts. Visit GAO on the web at www.gao.gov.
To Report Fraud, Waste, and Abuse in Federal Programs	Contact: Website: http://www.gao.gov/fraudnet/fraudnet.htm E-mail: fraudnet@gao.gov Automated answering system: (800) 424-5454 or (202) 512-7470
Congressional Relations	Katherine Siggerud, Managing Director, siggerudk@gao.gov, (202) 512-4400, U.S. Government Accountability Office, 441 G Street NW, Room 7125, Washington, DC 20548
Public Affairs	Chuck Young, Managing Director, youngc1@gao.gov, (202) 512-4800 U.S. Government Accountability Office, 441 G Street NW, Room 7149 Washington, DC 20548